Glasgow

Locomotive Builder to the World

Murdoch Nicolson, Mark O'Neill

Polygon Books
Third Eye Centre   Springburn Museum
Glasgow District Libraries Publications Board
1987

Glasgow: Locomotive Builder to the World

Published in an edition of 2,150 copies, August 1987

Edited by Christopher Carrell, Murdoch Nicolson, Mark O'Neill
Designed by Christopher Carrell
Published by Polygon Books (Edinburgh), Third Eye Centre (Glasgow), Springburn Museum, Glasgow District Libraries Publications Board
Distributed by Polygon Books, 48 The Pleasance, Edinburgh.
Tel: 031 558 1117
Printed by Peterson Printers, 12 Laygate, South Shields, Tyne and Wear
Third Eye Centre (Glasgow) Ltd is subsidised by the Scottish Arts Council and Glasgow District Council

ISBN 0 948275 46 4

Title page: *Gourock artist, George Wyllie's* The Straw Locomotive *suspended from the Finnieston Crane, May 1987. Photograph: George Oliver*

Below: *Spanish National Railways 2–8–2 passing the entrance to the pedestrian tunnel under the Clyde, c 1950*

Acknowledgements

This book arose out of George Wyllie's *The Straw Locomotive*, which was selected from open competition for the Glasgow site — the Finnieston Crane — of the TSWA 3D nationwide sited art works project. Chris Carrell, Director of Third Eye Centre, suggested that there was a need for a historical work on the subject of Glasgow's locomotive building industry. As well as creating the opportunity to publish these important photographs, he gave us constant encouragement, *and* designed the book. We were greatly aided by the unfailingly helpful staff of The Mitchell Library. Mr Miller (Director of Libraries), and Mr R McFarlane (Administrative Services) made the book possible by agreeing to co-publish it and by making available the Library's resources. Mr J Irvine (Photographic Department) did herculean work printing the photographs and Mr I Gordon (Science and Technology) and Mr M Moss (Glasgow University Archives) greatly helped us with our researches. Acknowledgement should be made here also to the North British Locomotive Company's official photographers, the last of whom were John Scott and Gordon Robertson, whose work is a lasting memorial to one of Glasgow's greatest industries.

Murdoch Nicolson
Technical Librarian
The Mitchell Library

Mark O'Neill
Curator
Springburn Museum

Contents

Note on the description of locomotives
The groups of three figures, such as 4–8–2 or 0–6–0, refer to the wheel arrangements, used to distinguish various types of locomotive. The centre figure is the number of driving wheels, ie the wheels driven by the piston rods. The leading and trailing wheels (first and last figures) are not driven. The gauge refers to the distance between the tracks of the railway for which the locomotive is designed.

Below: The Straw Locomotive *passing the derelict entrance to the closed pedestrian tunnel, 4 May 1987. Photograph: George Oliver*

The Companies

Walter Montgomerie Neilson and the Origins of Locomotive Building in Glasgow

Above: *Walter Montgomerie Neilson 1819–1880*

Below: *Neilson's new works at Hyde Park, Springburn*

The story of locomotive building in Glasgow began in the 1830s when a number of engineering firms tried their hands at making the new engines. It was not however until 1844 that the Neilsons' firm, which was to become the largest builder of locomotives in Britain, entered the field. For the next fifty years locomotive building in Glasgow was dominated by three men — Walter Neilson, Henry Dubs and James Reid. The two latter men began as employees of Neilson but went on to control their own works. The three works they managed were amalgamated in 1903 to form the largest locomotive manufacturing firm in Europe. Though the financial records of the early period have not survived we are extremely fortunate that Neilson's unpublished memoirs have. The insight they give into the men who founded and developed one of Glasgow's greatest industries is unique in the city's commercial history.

Walter Neilson was born in Glasgow in 1819. The firm he made famous began as an engineering works in Hyde Park Street, Finnieston, founded in 1836 by his cousin William Neilson and James Mitchell. It was in large part financed by Walter's father, James Beaumont Neilson, who was at this time working on his 'Hot Blast' method of manufacturing iron. In 1838 Walter joined the firm to complete an apprenticeship he had begun in the St Rollox Foundry Co. In about 1840 both William Neilson and James Mitchell left, dissolving the company. Walter's father and Stewart Kerr formed a new company, which "did excellent work in large factory driving engines" and built the engine for hauling locomotives up the Cowlairs Incline on the new Edinburgh and Glasgow Railway. However this work was carried out "always at a loss" and the company ran into financial difficulties. "At this time it was seriously under consideration to break up the whole works, as several attempts to sell the works as a going concern had not been successful". In 1843 Walter, then 24 years of age, was prevailed upon by the family solicitor, Dr Kirkwood, to take the business "into my own hands". James Mitchell returned from Liverpool to manage the financial side of the business, insisting, somewhat to Walter Neilson's annoyance, on becoming a partner. The firm was known as Neilson & Mitchell until 1855, when it was renamed Neilson & Co.

Walter Neilson described his decision to take up locomotive building as follows: "Seeing the number of Railways that were being made in Scotland and every thing for them got in England I determined to try to get some of the work for Scotland. I engaged William Tait as Foreman over the engine department, more particularly the Railway and Locomotive department in 1844". Apart from three locomotives for the Glasgow and Garnkirk Railway the first engines they built were small mineral tank engines for collieries which "were a very good thing for us". The business does seem to have prospered as it soon expanded: "In 1845 ground at Finnieston Street was bought and a new foundry commenced to be built — the old foundry at Hyde Park Street was then converted into a tool shop for locomotive engine making". Neilson's first export locomotive was for the Julian de Zulusta Railway, Havana in 1852. This probably arose from contacts established through supplying sugar making machinery to Cuba. The first order for Canada, for the Nova Scotia Railway, came two years later in 1854 and for India in 1859.

The company continued to build much else besides locomotives — "land engines, high pressure condensing engines, pumping engines, double cylinder engines, marine engines...sugar making Mills and machinery, Mining, pumping, Gas and Water machinery etc etc all going on together". By 1852 Neilson "felt satisfied that I could do no good in continuing to take orders for such a variety of works...I made up my mind that I must confine myself to some speciality and the choice seemed to be between Marine or Locomotive work." He was angered by the advice of friends who suggested that, just as the Clyde was the place for building steamers, locomotives were an English speciality and "if I intended to give myself up to Locomotive making, I ought to go to England, about Manchester. My reply to this always was, that if they could not be made in Glasgow and by Scotch workmen too, they would never be made by me in England". Elsewhere Neilson avowed his intention

Above: *Henry Dubs 1816–1876*

not "to employ a single Englishman". However, Manchester was to play a crucial part in Neilson's and Glasgow's locomotive-building history. Not only was it the base of rival manufacturers and a source of experience for Neilson employees but it was also the home of the firm which eventually rescued his second, ailing locomotive works.

Neilson did not implement his decision "to give myself up to locomotive engine making exclusively" for a number of years. Two major problems had to be overcome. First he needed "a manager for my works who had some name and reputation for this department of engineering . . . At this time a german (sic) Henry Dubs was strongly recommended to me, as a man in great favour and estimation by locomotive superintendants, and as likely to be of great value to me. Dubs was out of employment, and pressed me much for the situation". Dubs had in fact recently been dismissed from Beyer, Peacock in Manchester. He was born in Darmstadt in Germany in 1816. After training in Mainz and Aix-le-Chapelle he visited England in 1836. He returned in 1842 and went to work for the Vulcan Foundry near Warrington. In 1857 Beyer was worried about the slack attitude in the works, including the manager, Dubs, who was "of a far more happy, easy temper than anyone", which may account for his dismissal later that year (Hills and Patrick 1982 p17).

Before appointing Dubs, Neilson had to deal with the fact that he already had a works manager, James Reid, who, however, had no locomotive experience. James Reid was born in Kilmaurs, in Ayrshire, in 1823. He served his apprenticeship in Airdrie and in the Kilmarnock Foundry Co. Between 1847 and 1851 he worked for Scott, Sinclair & Co and Caird & Co, Greenock. "I was unwilling to part with Mr Reid, but was convinced that it would be to my interest to put Mr Dubs in his place". Reid was duly replaced and went to work for Sharp, Stewart & Co in Manchester. Neilson recalled, "I made Mr Dubs a partner, it having been always a principle with me that those whom I employed in any undertaking should not only have a sufficient salary, but also an interest in the undertaking", a belief he must have acquired since his dealings with James Mitchell, whose insistence on being a partner he resented.

His second problem was orders. He attributed the shortage of these to the English monopoly — "The prejudice against me in England was so strong that I would never have succeeded had it not been for the orders for Scotch Railways". Though Neilson had employed Dubs in part because of "his influence with those who could be the means of bringing orders to me" he found this method of getting orders distasteful in practice. "He had many friends amongst the locomotive superintendants, but I did not think the means he employed amongst those he could influence in favour of inducing orders to be given to us, were such as I could ever approve of as being honest and honourable and on this point he and I were never in accord".

The New Works at Springburn

The demand for engines, however it came about, was sufficiently encouraging for Neilson to decide to establish a new works. He selected a site to the north east of Glasgow in the village of Springburn. There were already two major locomotive works there, the Cowlairs Works (1841) owned by the Edinburgh and Glasgow Railway and the Caledonian Railway's St Rollox Works (1856). There was nonetheless the space he needed and Neilson bought a site half way between the two existing works. He may also have been attracted by the proximity of main railway lines for convenient delivery to the British market. As the firm came more and more to rely on export business the engines had to be brought back to Finnieston for shipping. The out-of-gauge engines had to be transported by road on low loaders, the sight of which is still a vivid memory for many Glaswegians, especially in Springburn.

Although the *Jubilee History of the North British Locomotive Company* (1953 p26) states that Dubs laid out the Springburn works, Neilson claims that he did so himself. "Land was purchased for new works at Springburn and it was not long before I had the plans and designs for them completed, because for some years before this time I had visited all the important works in Europe and America and taken advantage of the information there obtained. I completed the designs of perhaps the most successful locomotive building establishment that had up to that time been built".

Machinery and equipment were transported to Springburn on horse-drawn wagons, aided by large numbers of the works employees. They walked in front of the wagons and hauled on long drag ropes. The *Jubilee History* (p26) describes the scene. "The gradients in High Street, Castle Street and Springburn Road presented formidable obstacles and a large crowd of interested spectators usually gathered to see the sight. Although no records exist it is traditionally believed that the steps taken to refresh the exhausted workers were more than adequate".

Between 1844 and 1862 Neilson built 429 locomotives at Finnieston, 68 of which went abroad. The first locomotive exported from the Springburn works was the 2–2–2 which Said Pasha saw at the London Exhibition and bought for Egypt, the first of many for that country. Among the countries the firm exported to were Argentina, Australia, Austria, Bechuanaland, Belgium, Benguela, Denmark, Egypt, France, Greece, Holland, Italy, Japan, Mauritius, Natal, New Zealand, Norway, Portugal, Rhodesia, Russia, South Africa, Spain, Sudan, Sweden and Turkey.

The disagreement about who laid out the works may reflect Neilson's growing disenchantment with Dubs who "turned out to be an excellent draughtsman, but was a poor engineer". Neilson judged him to be "a most pig headed german (sic) and a most difficult man to get along with". The example Neilson gives to justify this charge does not reflect well on either of them but gives us a good picture of the relationship between owner and manager; "each line of gearing was driven directly by an independant (sic) steam engine, as I would not have any tooth gearing in the works, — it was consequently necessary that these independant steam engines should each have a most sensitive governor (a device which ensured that the engine ran at a constant speed) and I gave a sketch of a new arrangement of a governor to Mr Dubs to be adopted in the works, but he said he could make a better governor so I did not object to his doing so, and after he and his German draughtsman had spent a considerable time and a good deal of money in scheming something different from what I recommended to him and had totally failed to make a governor suitable for the purpose, I peremptorily told him that now I must have the governor made on my plan to be tried. This he positively refused to do, telling me, he would not make it and I might do so if I desired. This governor turned out to be most successful, greatly to the annoyance and disgust of Mr Dubs".

Dubs Goes It Alone

It is hardly surprising in these circumstances that Neilson and Dubs soon parted company. "Dubs made himself so excessively disagreeable and having offered to give up his partnership and leave the works upon my paying him a certain sum of money, which I accepted... I knew Mr Dubs would find friends to assist him to build new works in Glasgow and I stipulated with him, that his new works he would build should not be nearer than 3 miles to the Hyde Park Works".

Below: *Hyde Park Works 1864. Breezes Tower (1830) and Springburn Parish Church (1842) in the background*

Above: *Ottoman Company (Turkey). This 12 horse-power traction engine was designed for road use and was built in 1866*

Dubs chose a site on the south side of Glasgow at Queen's Park in Polmadie. The first sod on the new works was cut in 1864 and within a year Dubs and Co had produced its first locomotive. The works was well equipped, with about 100 machine tools costing £16,467 being bought from Whitworth and Co in Manchester. The Dubs and Co works plate was triangular in shape and was derived from the mark on the bricks of which the new works were built. Dubs took a number of key workers with him to Queen's Park, including Sampson George Goodall-Copestake, Neilson's chief draughtsman, who went on to become a partner in the firm. It is also apparent from the company's order books that many of Neilson's customers placed orders with Dubs, who must have used his 'many friends' to good advantage. Dubs received his first foreign orders in 1866, for the unusual Ottoman Railway traction engine and East Indian Railway locomotives. The list of countries to which engines were subsequently sold is as impressive as Neilson's.

In January 1866, Dubs and Co became one of the first engineering firms to employ women in its drawing office as tracers. Up to this time women had not been considered capable of doing this type of work, and objections were raised on these grounds, as well as on the grounds of propriety.

Dubs died in 1876 and William Lorimer, who had joined the firm in 1864, became managing partner. He became first chairman of the North British Locomotive Company in 1903. By that time Dubs and Co employed 2,423 men and was the second largest locomotive works in Britain.

Neilson and Reid Split

In 1850 Neilson described James Reid as having "always been a kind friend to me". Nor does Reid seem to have resented being replaced by Dubs for, in 1863, he returned to Neilson & Co Neilson later wrote "I took back my old foreman, James Reid, who had been with Sharp, Stewart & Co. at Manchester ever since he left me. Mr Reid I knew from experience to be a very superior man as an engineer to Mr Dubs and now that he had experience of locomotive-making at Sharp, Stewart & Co's place, I was satisfied he was the very man for me and took him as a partner for 10 years".

Below: *James Reid 1823–1894*

In about 1872, when the period of Reid's partnership was coming to an end they had a disagreement which left Neilson very bitter. As we do not have Reid's version of events Neilson's is our only account and must therefore be read with caution:

"The Hyde Park Locomotive Works rather were doing as well as I expected, still we had some bad years and as I did not intend to continue all my lifetime in this business and Mr Reid was not a man of capital but a most excellent manager and a man who looked keenly to his own business. I ultimately in extending my partnership with him gave him the option on very favourable terms of bying (sic) me out altogether, which he did, but not on the terms I had intended in the contract that was made with him by Dr Kirkwood. He having been with me at the old works knew very well the great sacrifice I had made in removing to the new works and as the new works had been proved to be very successfull (sic) and profitable of which he got his share, my understanding always that he would pay me a fair and liberal price for the old machinery, but by some flaws of Dr Kirkwood's contract it turned out that he could demand the purchase of the new works and the old tools all together at an arbitrator's value. The umpire for the valuation was a Mr Walter Patterson, the others named in the contract having died. This Patterson was a little pedantic, empty headed creature, whom I had often seen in Glasgow and indeed had quite forgotten that he was to be our umpire in Neilson and Co's affairs and so rather avoided becoming intimate with him, one of the many mistakes I made in my life. Mr Reid acted more wisely by cultivating his friendship and preparing for using him to his advantage, as it turned out, that the arbitor Walter Patterson acted entirely under Mr Reid's instructions. This had gone on for years and Dr Kirkwood got so disgusted with the case that he threw it up and placed me in a very awkward position and in fact did not treat me as I thought with much consideration seeing he had this case all along from the beginning, even the working out of the contract of the partnership with Mr Reid. Mr Bannatyne now looked after the case but it seems I could not get out of the hands in which Dr Kirkwood had allowed me to be caught and it was of course not the least likely that Mr Reid would give up a tool that worked so easily in his hands and took every care to employ it in taking every shilling out of my pocket that was possible for him to do. This was the thanks I got for taking a young man, James Reid from Caird and Co's drawing office, employed there for a few shillings a week wages and making him my foreman or manager at Hyde Park St and then a partner at my works at Springburn".

This leaves a number of questions unanswered so that one feels that it is not, to say the least, a complete account of the events. The question of what precisely "had been going on for a number of years" which had so disgusted Dr Kirkwood is answered in a note in the margin — he found "himself in the position of being treated

Above: *Visit of Marquis Tseng, Envoy Extraordinary & Minister Plenipotentiary of H M the Emperor of China, to Hyde Park Works in 1886. Hugh Reid, son of James Reid, is third from the left. Sir William McOnie, Lord Provost of Glasgow, is in the centre, next to Marquis Tseng. The engine is an Indian State Railway 4–6–0, one of 50 built by Neilson & Co in 1885–6, 5′ 6″ gauge*

Below: *Visit of Li Hung Chang to Hyde Park Works, 18 August 1896. Hugh Reid is standing in the cab. By this time James Reid had died and the firm was managed by his sons. The engine is a Midland & Great Northern Joint Committee 0–6–0. 8 were built in 1896*

Above: *Pernambuco Railway (Brazil) 0–6–0T built for Dick, Kerr & Co in 1887, 2′ 0″ gauge*

not as a straightforward and honourable adviser, but as one being driven into a corner by Mr Reid's unjust demands and statements, always supported by this Mr Patterson, from whom it seems there was no possibility of escape". According to Neilson's memoirs Dr Kirkwood had been the family legal and financial adviser since at least 1843. It seems unlikely that we shall ever know if Kirkwood's desertion was prompted or justified by something Neilson himself did: if it was not, Dr Kirkwood does seem to have treated Neilson very badly indeed.

However this was not the end of Neilson's tale of woe: "Another part of this arrangement that turned out so unfavourable to me was that I agreed to give up my share of the business for . . . . years payment of the average profit of 4 years partnership and unfortunately these last few years of partnership turned out to be the worst that Neilson and Co ever have had. The result being that this most valuable business was given away to Mr Reid for a mere nothing-...So far as my memory goes although I never made up the sum exactly, I considered I was being robbed by Mr Reid of a sum equal to £20,000." It seems strange that Neilson could not remember, or was reluctant to write down, the number of years profit he was to receive. However underneath Neilson's sense of betrayal, there seems to be a respect for Reid which he did not feel for Dubs, along with perhaps envy of what he perceived to be Reid's ruthlessness and cunning.

The net result of this conflict was that Reid had complete control of Neilson and Co by 1876. He continued as sole partner until 1893, when he was joined by four of his sons, Hugh (who became senior partner), Andrew, John and Walter. He died the following year, in the words of the *Jubilee History* (1953 p28) "on St Andrew's golf course on the 23rd June 1894, after a valiant but vain attempt to play his ball from a difficult lie in a bunker". The firm was renamed Neilson, Reid and Co in 1898. By the time of the amalgamation of the three firms in 1903 it was the largest locomotive works in Britain and employed 3,410 men.

The Clyde Locomotive Company

Neilson spent much of the 1870s and '80s abroad but in 1884 he established the Clyde Locomotive Company, and built new works just across the railway line from the Hyde Park Works. Unfortunately his memoirs are silent about his 'comeback' and we can only speculate on his motives for setting up this company and the challenging location of its works. Neilson had difficulty in getting orders however, and in the first two years of operation, 1886/7, he built only 23 locomotives. Six of these were for export, one for the Eglinton Iron Co in Santander in Spain and five for a Brazilian railway.

Sharp, Stewart and Co Takeover

Once again Manchester was the source of a decisive intervention in Glasgow's locomotive building affairs. Sharp, Stewart & Co, who had been building locomotives in that city since 1834 were looking for a new works, as their Atlas Works had no room for expansion. It was also not convenient to railway sidings or docks. They were therefore attracted to Glasgow by the site of the Clyde Locomotive Company Works and by the lower wages and rates prevailing in Scotland. In 1888 Neilson sold the principal interest in his company to Sharp, Stewart who renamed it the Atlas Works after their old works in Manchester. In their Manchester period Sharp, Stewart had built 3,442 locomotives, of which an estimated 2,275 were exported. Neilson's order E6 for eight locomotives for the Brazilian Government Railway, was transferred to Sharp, Stewart, who completed it. Between 1888 and 1903 the company built 1,646 locomotives, an average of 110 a year, though it had the capacity to build 150. By the time of the amalgamation it employed 1,737 men and was the third largest locomotive works in Britain, just ahead of Beyer, Peacock of Manchester.

Mark O'Neill

Below:
Mount Lyell Railway (Tasmania) 0–4–2T. This rack and adhesion system engine was built in 1896, 3′ 6″ gauge

The Companies II

The North British Locomotive Company

In 1903 the North British Locomotive Company was formed by the amalgamation of Neilson Reid & Co, Dubs & Co and Sharp, Stewart & Co. The union of the three largest locomotive building firms in Britain caused consternation among other British builders but talk of taking legal action to prevent it came to nothing. The new company was the largest locomotive building firm in Europe, or indeed anywhere outside America. It employed 7,570 men and was capable of producing over 600 locomotives a year. It was hoped that by ceasing to compete with each other and by benefitting from the economies of large scale production, the Glasgow firms would be better able to combat competition from America, Germany and from other British firms. However, these advantages were not sufficient to avert trouble, signs of which were present even before 1914. Output never reached capacity — the peak was 573 engines in 1905. Though an average of 529.5 engines a year were built between 1904 and 1909, the 1909 total was less than 400 and the 1910 total below 300. The fewer the engines produced, the more expensive each one became. This made the company, with its huge overheads, less and less able to compete. The outbreak of war in 1914 however created a great demand for locomotives and for the armaments which the company began to manufacture in vast quantities.

The post-war boom in demand reached its high point in 1920, when 307 engines were built. This level was never reached again before World War II. In 1922 there was a sharp drop with only 97 engines being built. The following year *The Indian & Eastern Engineer*, published in Calcutta, wrote: "We regret to notice . . that the North British Locomotive Company Limited has had to dispense with the services of a considerable number of its workmen engaged at the Atlas Works...For some time now the company has succeeded in keeping its three works...in something like fair employment by distributing the orders received among them. That policy apparently can no longer be continued, and it had become necessary to concentrate the work in hand at two of the establishments. The Atlas Works will not be completely closed down. The directors express the hope that in the near future trade will improve to an extent permitting the company to resume its operation on the usual scale, and give employment to its workmen, many of whom have been in its service since boyhood". The Works was advertised for sale in the *Glasgow Herald* in 1927 but no buyer was found, though most of the machine tools were auctioned off. The average annual production for the 1920s was 183 engines. The directors assumed that it was another of the cyclical depressions which affected heavy engineering firms, especially those dependent on the export market. But there were still worse times to come. The Great Depression, which began in 1929, caused a worldwide collapse of the demand for locomotives — in 1933 the company built only 16 engines and the average for 1930/38 was 62 a year. To make matters worse, in order to retain a core of skilled workers many of the locomotives were sold at a loss, including every one of the 225 engines sold to Egypt between the wars.

The annual reports in the 1920s and 1930s list the reasons for the poor state of the company — the high value of the pound compared to the German Mark made its engines more expensive; a growth in protectionism, for example in Australia; a policy of favouring local manufacturers among former customers, even among the Dominions, such as India. Many manufacturing countries, as well as protecting their industries by tariff barriers, subsidised them. In these circumstances the NBL found it very difficult to compete — even tendering at a loss did not work and an Egyptian contract was lost to Italy, to the Board's annoyance and disbelief. The key factor in the decline was however simply the drop in international demand for locomotives. In spite of these difficulties the Board offered no other tactic for dealing with the depression other than to wait for it to go away. It is not clear what they could have done and one business historian has expressed "sympathy with the view that the catastrophic collapse of their traditional markets virtually provided a problem beyond their power to solve" (Campbell 1978 p213) and suggests that the company survived as long as it did only because of its strong financial reserves built up during more prosperous days.

NBL was revived however by the outbreak of the Second World War in 1939 and the boom which followed. In 1947 the Chairman of the company, Sir Frederick C Stewart, told the Annual General

Below: *Neilson's second Springburn works, taken over by Sharp, Stewart & Co and renamed the Atlas Works in 1888. In 1903 it became part of the North British Locomotive Company*

Meeting that "our order book is well filled, and not forgetting the effects on cost and production of the 44 hours week, we can compete with success in the world's markets". In 1948 Sir Frederick announced that during the past year they had reached an agreement with the General Electric Company to co-operate with them in the manufacture of electric and diesel locomotives and had already received orders for both of these types. They also developed a special type of diesel locomotive for underground haulage in mines, and had orders in hand for a quantity of these from clients at home and abroad. 1948 was also the year the North British Locomotive Company (Africa) Ltd was established, a 'small subsidiary' to look after the company's interests in this 'great market'. In these promising circumstances the Atlas Works was reopened for locomotive production.

Another encouraging development in 1948 was the prospect of a large order of locomotives for Russia. This work was being undertaken "at the request of His Majesty's Government". This fell through because, according to the only cutting from *The Daily Worker* in the NBL's scrapbook, the Board of Trade refused export licences for "possible Soviet orders for 1,250 and of Chinese orders for 500". In the year of the emergence of the Cold War with the Communist coup in Czechoslovakia and the Berlin blockade this is a reasonable interpretation of events.

In spite of this setback the boom continued, though in 1952 the NBL's results were 'disappointing' when compared to Robert Stephenson & Hawthorns and Beyer, Peacock & Co. From 1956 the company was again operating at a loss. Early in 1958 the Chairman J B Mavor promised a return to profitability if nothing unforeseen occurred. "This further change for the better results from the fact that the re-equipment of the works for the production of diesel in place of steam locomotives is complete and the company had secured major contracts for diesel types (mainly diesel hydraulic) from the British Transport Commission". Later that year however he had to report that "difficulties have unfortunately been experienced in building up production of the higher powered North British/MAN diesel engines and the North British Voith transmissions, which have delayed the completion of the locomotives".

1959 saw a major downturn in NBL's fortunes — "Our biggest customer (the British Transport Commission) has decided no longer to make progressive payments in respect of new contracts". The company's poor position meant that the money necessary to continue in operation could not be raised on the open market. The directors accordingly borrowed £1.75 million from the Treasury, £500,000 'from our friends, the G.E.C.' and £1.75 million from banks. They received permission from their shareholders to borrow another £5 million if they thought it necessary.

The problems with the conversion to diesel continued and in 1960 they failed to get a share of the BTC's order for 200 diesel engines. On 19 October *The Daily Express* reported the NBL's Chairman, Mr Thomas Coughtrie, as saying: "I do not blame the Transport Commission for taking a dim view of the North British Locomotive Company. They had some bitter experience with our products". He maintained that if it had not been for "bad workmanship on stock already completed or found faulty on inspection, the firm might have been showing a profit this year". This statement can have done nothing for the morale of a workforce struggling to acquire new skills under the NBL's reputedly haphazard retraining scheme.

Overseas as well as British orders were drastically down and in April 1962 the *Glasgow Herald* reported that the company was about to close. An editorial summarised the causes of its decline and the efforts to halt it. "Two of the ablest business men in the country – Mr Thomas Coughtrie and Lord Reith – were appointed to the Board, and strenuous efforts were made to diversify the company's own products and enable it to hold its own against increasing competition from home and overseas makers of diesel and electric locomotives. But the employees were still 'steam-minded' and it proved impossible to adapt them quickly enough to the demands of precision engineering. As Lord Polworth said last night, 'They failed to see the writing on the wall in time.' Most of the firm's competitors saw the writing on the wall at the end of the Second World War. Some of them appreciated that steam might be supplanted by other forms of railway traction".

Given the long and highly specialised apprenticeships and the policy of employing successive generations of the same family it was understandable that the workers were 'steam-minded'. It seems unfair to blame them for the firm's collapse however as they had never been permitted to participate in decision-making at any level. As late as 1922 Sir Hugh Reid, the Deputy Chairman of NBL, asserted the right of management to perform "those functions which could only be exercised properly by employers and their officials without the interference of unions". This autocratic view of labour relations did nothing to increase the company's flexibility. The management also showed signs of steam-mindedness. In 1936, even after 16 years of more or less continuous trade recession, Mr William Lorimer asserted that "the era of the steam locomotive was by no means over, 'pointing out that' for long-distance main-line transport no machine had yet been devised which excelled the steam locomotive for efficiency, economy and reliability". This inertia was reinforced by the traditionally passive management response to trade depressions and by the temporary booms brought about by two world wars.

The combination of the company's limited capacity to respond positively to change and its heavy dependence on an export market which could not last proved fatal. The liquidation was formally announced on 19 April 1962. Redundancies had begun in 1960 and overall some 5,000 men lost their jobs. For over a hundred years Glasgow, and especially Springburn, had been a major exporter of Scottish engineering to all parts of the world. The ultimate failure of the company does not diminish the justifiable pride felt by those who inherited a tradition of skill the equal of any in the industrialized world.

Mark O'Neill

Below: *Boiler Pit, Queen's Park Works. After each level of the boiler was rivetted it was lowered into the pit so that the next area to be worked was within reach. The boiler is from a South African Railways 15C locomotive. 29 were built at Queen's Park in 1928, 3' 6" gauge*

The Locomotives

The locomotive output of the North British Locomotive Company and its constituents reflects virtually every aspect of development from the days of the introduction of the railways up to the 1960s. As the locomotive progressed from the primitive forms which were first in operation, so the companies progressed in their manufacturing techniques. They were always among the leading innovators in the field, especially with regard to locomotives built for overseas railways which were setting up their systems from scratch. Because of Britain's unique position in the profligation of railways, many of these new methods were first used on the home railways. The Glasgow firms had a substantial share of the home market and were able to incorporate the technical improvements into their exported engines.

Because of physical geographical difficulties, such as mountainous country in South America and in certain parts of India, the vast distances and arid areas of Africa, and the location on the coast of the main centres of population in Australia, the North British Locomotive Company and its predecessors were asked to solve many problems not often encountered in the home countries. Many overseas railways varied from the standard 4′ 8½″ gauge of railway track adopted in Britain, so technical improvements made in Britain had to be adapted to the constrictions of differing rail widths and loading gauges. The range of locomotives built included the 2′ 0″ examples for the mountainous Darjeeling-Himalayan Railway of India, the vast numbers of metre gauge locomotives for other railways in India, the 3′ 6″ engines for lines in many parts of Africa, the many standard gauge engines for countries such as Egypt and China and the 5′ 6″ gauge engines used on many main lines in India. In addition to meeting the demands of public railway networks, many locomotives were also built for industrial concerns throughout the world, such as those used for hauling ore trains from various African gold mines or on sugar plantations. Those supplied to major railways ranged from prestigious main line express engines, with the emphasis on speed, through the powerful locomotives required for hauling extremely heavy goods trains over long distances, the smaller tender and tank engines used for suburban and branch line traffic, to the small shunting engines used primarily in railway yards. While it is not possible to examine all these in detail here, the following gives some idea of the engineering achievements of Glasgow's private locomotive builders.

Sharp, Stewart & Co

The firm of Sharp, Roberts, later Sharp Brothers, and finally Sharp, Stewart & Co, originally founded in Manchester in 1822, built large numbers of locomotives before moving to Glasgow in 1888. These included approximately 600 2–2–2s, built between 1837 and 1857, which became known as the 'Sharp Single' and were in effect standard locomotives suitable for all types of work. Size of cylinder and driving wheel varied, but otherwise the locomotives were almost identical. Many were supplied to British railways but they were also exported to France, Italy, Spain, Belgium, Denmark, Holland, Germany and Russia. Another locomotive which became a standard, and was built by Sharp, Stewart well into the early years of the North British Locomotive Company, was the F Class 0–6–0, large numbers of which were supplied to various Indian railways. These were also built by Neilson & Co and Dubs & Co. Again cylinder sizes and driving wheel diameters varied.

Among the most unusual locomotives built by Sharp, Stewart in their Manchester period was a batch of fifteen for the Lisbon Tramways in 1872. They had the improbable wheel arrangement of 1–1–2D–1–1. The Lisbon Tramways operated on a single rail system and the locomotives had two single wheels behind each other at each end which ran on the central rail. Two 11″x18″ cylinders drove two driving wheels of 3′ 9″ diameter which were not flanged and ran on the road alongside the single rail.

After the move to Glasgow, Sharp, Stewart continued to build many locomotives for foreign railways, including a batch of five 4–6–0s for the metre gauge Mogyana Railway, Brazil, and nine 4–4–0s for the standard gauge Dutch Rhenish Railway. The last foreign contract before amalgamation was for five 2–8–0 locomotives for the metre gauge Leopoldina Railway, Brazil.

Neilson & Co

Neilson & Co, founded as Mitchell and Neilson in 1836 and undergoing several name changes before finally becoming Neilson, Reid & Co in 1898, also built large numbers of locomotives for foreign railways. One of their earlier products of a more unusual design was an ice locomotive supplied to Russia in 1861, works number 786. It did not run on rails but on frozen snow and had a single pair of driving wheels, 5′ 0″ in diameter with steel spokes projecting from the rims. These were driven by two cylinders of dimension 10″ x 22″ via an intermediate shaft on which were the eccentrics connected to the driving wheels by coupling rods. The front of the engine was carried on a sprung sleigh. It had no cab, like many conventional examples of the period, which must have been unpleasant for the person firing the locomotive, especially during the Russian winters. As it did not run on rails, it had to be steered by means of a spoked wheel, rather like that to be found on a ship, situated on a platform in front of the chimney. The steering position was entirely unprotected from the elements except for a casing in front which came to about waist height. The person doing the steering must thus have been even worse off than the fireman, who could at least get a certain amount of heat from the firebox. The engine weighed twelve tons in working order. It carried out a regular mail and passenger service between St Petersburg and Cronstadt, hauling a train of three railway coaches mounted on sleigh irons. The track was kept clear and provided with telegraph wires and signals. Sometimes the engine also travelled into the country on sleigh roads.

Like the other firms, Neilson & Co exhibited examples of their products at public exhibitions and trade fairs visited by representatives from every type of business from all over the world. In 1862, at the London Exhibition, the firm exhibited a 2–2–2 tender locomotive with 8′ 2″ driving wheels. The locomotive was bought by the Said Pasha of Egypt who wanted an engine which "could travel at 70 miles per hour". Two similar engines were ordered in 1865 and the three remained in service for about thirty years. These engines give some indication of what railway locomotives were capable of in the 1860s.

In 1886 the Hyde Park Works supplied two 0–4–2T locomotives to the New Zealand Government Railways. These were Fell type locomotives which had rack and adhesion propulsion and were for use on the exceptionally steep Rimutaka Incline, which was of 3′ 6″ gauge. They had outside cylinders which drove the conventional flanged driving wheels when the engines were in use on the flatter part of the line. On the steep inclines a toothed rack rail was laid between the tracks. When the engines reached these sections similarly toothed driving wheels, horizontally spring loaded and driven by two inside cylinders, were engaged. This helped the engines haul their trains up the steep sections where the ordinary wheels would have had difficulty in gripping and would have slipped excessively. Neilson supplied other examples of these engines as separate orders.

In addition to these unusual engines a great variety of locomotives of the more conventional type were supplied to railways all over the world for many different purposes. The last foreign order before the firm lost its individual identity was for the thirty 4–8–0 tender locomotives supplied to the 3′ 6″ gauge Central South African Railway.

Top right: *Darjeeling-Himalayan Railway B Class 0–4–0T in service. One built at Queen's Park Works in 1927, 2′ 0″ gauge*

Middle right: *Mogyana Railway (Brazil) 4–6–0. One built by Sharp, Stewart & Co in 1888, metre gauge*

Bottom right: *Dutch Rhenish Railway 4–4–0. One of 9 built in 188?, 4′ 8½″ gauge*

D.H.R.

51
COMPANHIA MOGYANA.

Top: *Corry Ice Engine. Built for Russia in 1861*

Above: *New Zealand Government Railway 0–4–2. One of 2 rack and adhesion engines built in 1886 at the Hyde Park Works, 3′ 6″ gauge. The rack ran between the two rails and was gripped by toothed wheels lowered from the engine. This enabled them to climb very steep inclines. Engine numbers 203,199 and 201 are here shown pulling the Royal Train on the famous Rimutaka Incline in New Zealand. More than one order of these was supplied*

Below: *Grand Trunk Railway of Canada 4–4–0. One of 25 built in 1868, 5′ 6″ gauge*

Above left: *Cape Government Railways 4–6–0. One of 37 built in 1895–7, 3′ 6″ gauge*

Above: *Compagnie de Midi (France) 2–4–0. One of 5 built in 1881, 4' 8½" gauge*

Below: *Boiler Shop, Hyde Park Works c1900*

Below: *Smithy, Hyde Park Works c1900. The large hydraulic press on the right was used for bending steel plate*

Below: *Light Machine Shop c1900. Cast and forged parts were machined here, ie. they were ground, filed or turned in lathes to make sure they fitted perfectly together*

Above: *Belgian State Railways 4–4–0. One of 5 built in 1898–9, 4′ 8½″ gauge*

Below: *Tracers at Hyde Park Works c1900*

Dubs & Co

Dubs & Co, founded in 1863, built many locomotives for railways in all parts of the world. Its engines gained a reputation for longevity and reliability, as proven by the two 2–4–2Ts supplied to the Bundaberg Railway, Queensland, Australia, in 1880 which survived up to 1947 and 1950 respectively; examples of the Dubs 4–10–2T and 4–8–2T engines originally supplied in the 1880s were seen in service in Africa as recently as 1980. However, the first locomotives Dubs sent to China in 1886, the *Speedy Peace* and *Flying Victory*, did not last very long. Although not the first locomotives seen in China, this pair of 0–4–0STs caused great trepidation among the local populace who claimed that the burial grounds of their ancestors were being desecrated. In an effort to stop the fire-breathing monsters, bound coolies were thrown in front of the engines to bring them to a halt. The trains were then overturned. After some 20 men had been given to the 'dragons' in this way the line was closed and the two locomotives scrapped.

The Turks had earlier been treated to the spectacle of a rather unusual Dubs machine dashing around the countryside. This was a four-wheeled steam traction engine named *Abdul Aziz*, built for the Ottoman Company in 1866. Like the Neilson ice engine it was controlled from a platform at the front of the engine and had a steering wheel like that on a ship.

Very few batches of locomotives were supplied to the North American Continent as firms such as Baldwin and the American Locomotive Company, the two largest manufacturers in the world, had a virtual monopoly in North America. European manufacturers faced the additional cost of having to ship their engines across the Atlantic ocean. Dubs & Co obtained a couple of orders from Canadian Railways. One of these was for 4–4–0s with driving wheels of 5′ 3″ diameter and 17″ x 24″ cylinders, built for the Canadian Pacific Railway in 1881. They looked like the type of locomotive to be seen in older western films, with spindly wheels and a large bulbous chimney necessary to prevent sparks from the exhaust setting fire to the dense forest areas through which some of the railway tracks ran. Like the other firms, Dubs & Co built many conventional engines, including a batch of three for Japan which was the last order before amalgamation.

Above: *Regla & Matanzas Railway (Cuba) 4–4–0. Built in 1886–7, 4′ 8½″ gauge*

Below: Flying Victory — *with* Speedy Peace *the first Glasgow engines supplied to China, in 1886, 1′ 11⅝″ gauge*

The North British Locomotive Company

The new North British Locomotive Company's first order, number L1, was placed in April 1903 by the Indian State Railways for their Eastern Bengal Railway. By March 1904 the five 4–6–0 locomotives, with 4′ 9″ driving wheels and 15½″ x 22″ outside cylinders, were completed. These engines were the first standard metre gauge 4–6–0s supplied to India. Between 1903 and its demise in 1962, NBL built steam tender locomotives of wheel arrangements 0–6–0, 0–8–0, 2–4–2, 2–6–0, 2–8–0, 2–10–0, 4–4–0, 4–4–2, 4–6–0, 4–6–2, 4–6–4, 4–8–0, 4–8–2 and 4–8–4, plus tank engines of wheel arrangement 0–4–0, 0–4–4, 0–6–0, 0–6–2, 0–6–4, 0–8–0, 0–8–2, 0–8–4, 2–4–0, 2–4–2, 2–6–0, 2–6–2, 2–6–4, 2–8–2, 2–8–4, 4–4–0, 4–4–2, 4–6–0, 4–6–2, 4–6–4 and 4–8–4. This excludes special types of locomotives such as Fairlies, Mallets, and Garratts with their complex and unusual wheel arrangements.

The reputation of the constituent firms for quality and reliability stood NBL in good stead for their export market. Apart from orders for British railways, locomotives were sent to every continent. In Africa NBL supplied locomotives to Egypt, the Gold Coast, Mashonaland, Natal, Nigeria, Nyasaland, Rhodesia, Sierra Leone, Sudan, Tanganyika,Transvaal, Uganda. In Southern Africa locomotives were supplied to Cape Government Railways, Central South African Railways, New Cape Central Railway and a large number of engines, around fifty orders, went to South African Railways. Apart from state railways, numerous industrial concerns purchased NBL locomotives: the Anglo-American Corporation, Tweefontein Collieries Ltd, Imperial Chemical Industries Ltd, West Reefs Exploration and Development Company Ltd, East Rand Proprietary Mines, St Helena Gold Mine and Vryheid Colliery. In the North American continent locomotives were supplied to the Canadian Pacific Railway and the Mexican State Railways, although none were built for the USA. The lion's share of the South American market went to the huge United States builders but European firms were also well represented, especially British and German builders. NBL supplied locomotives to Argentinian railways such as the Buenos Ayres and Pacific Railway, the Buenos Ayres Midland Railway, the Buenos Ayres Great Southern Railway and the Entre Rios Railway: to Brazilian railways such as the Leopoldina Railway, the San Paulo Railway, and the Great Western of Brazil Railway: and to various railways in Chile, Bolivia, Peru and Uruguay. Among the locomotives supplied to Asia were vast numbers for the Indian subcontinent, where customers included the Assam Railways and Trading Company, Bengal Nagpur Railway, Bengal and North Western Railway, Bhavnagar State Railway, Bombay Baroda and Central India Railway, Burma Railway Company, Burma Mines, Calcutta Port Commission, Ceylon Railways, Darjeeling Himalayan Railway, East Indian Railway, Great Indian Peninsula Railway, Porbander State Railway, the various components of the Indian State Railways, the Jodhpur Bikanir Railway, Kalka Simla Railway, Karachi Port Trust, Madras Railway, Nizam's Guaranteed State Railway, Rohilkund and Kumaon Railway, South Indian Railway, Junagad State Railway, Jamnnagar and Dwarka Railway, and the Indian Stores Department. Orders were supplied to China for railways such as the Canton Kowloon Railway, the Imperial Chinese Railways, the King Kan Railway, the Shanghai Northern Railway, the Shanghai Hangchow Ningpo Railway, the Tientsin Pukow Railway,and the Peiping Liaoning Railway. Other Asian countries to receive locomotives from NBL were Japan, Taiwan, Malaya and Siam (Thailand).

Australia also brought a fair income to the NBL, with engines supplied to the Metropolitan Coal Company Sydney, New South Wales Government Railways, Queensland Government Railways, South Australian Government Railways, Western Australian Goldfields Supply Company, Western Australian Millar's Karri and Jarrah Company (1902) Ltd, Western Australian Government Railways, and Victorian Railways. Engines also went to New Zealand and Tasmanian railway companies.

Among NBL's European customers were France, Palestine, Portugal and Spain. Spanish customers included the Andalous Railway Company, the Great Southern Railway of Spain, the Cia Minera de Sierra Menera, the Rio Tinto Railway, RENFE (Spanish National Railways), the San Martin Railway, the Santander and Bilbao Railway, the Tharsis Sulphur and Copper Company and the Vasco Asturiano Railway. The supply to other European countries had decreased since the amalgamation, the constituent firms had also supplied orders to Russia, Germany, Belgium, Holland, and all the Scandinavian countries. They had also laid down the ground work for North British, and it should be remembered that the sterling work done by the three constituent firms in gaining reputations for quality and reliability stood the larger amalgamation in good stead for winning the many orders necessary to keep its large work force employed.

Below: *Canadian Pacific Railways 4–6–0, one of 20 built at the Hyde Park Works in 1903, 4′ 8½″ gauge. One of the few orders for the North American continent*

Above: *Hyde Park Works (bottom) and Atlas Works (above) in the 1950s*

Below: *Atlas Works Erecting Shop, c1910 see written caption on left*

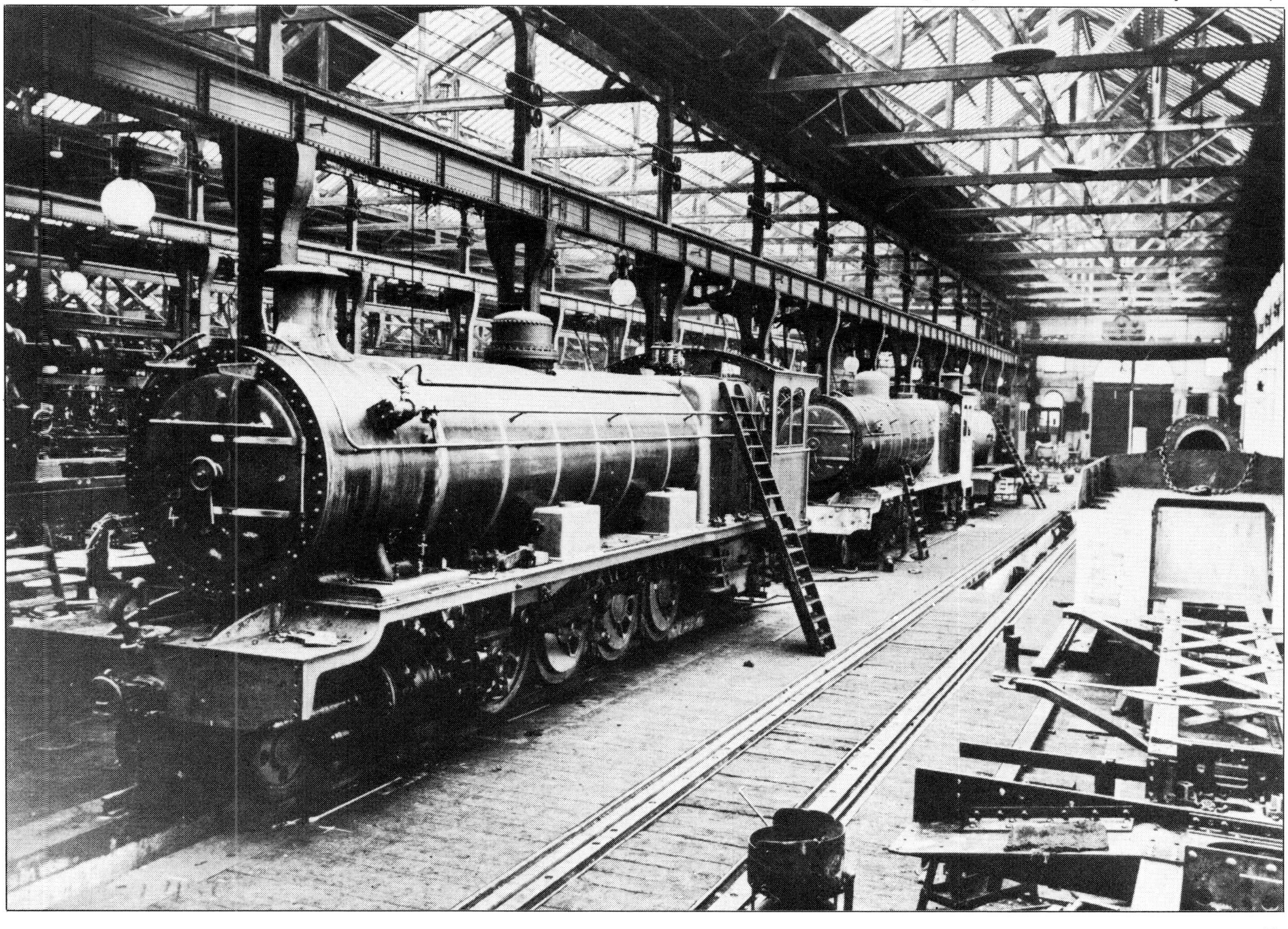

Above: *Paris-Orleans Railway (France) 2–8–2T. One of 30 built in Queen's Park Works, 1915–6. 1439.9mm gauge*

Below: *Queen's Park Works, c1950*

Above: *King Kan Railway (China) 0–8–0. One of 6 built at Hyde Park Works in 1936, 4′ 8½″ gauge*

Below: *Steam Hammers, Queen's Park Works, 1925. These massive hammers were used to forge axles*

Above: *Visit of Kabaka of Uganda to North British Locomotive Company's Hyde Park Works*

Below: *South African Railways 2–6–6–0 Mallet compound, 3′ 6″ gauge*

Below: *Central Argentine Railway CS class 4–8–0. One of 20 built in 1945–8, 5′ 6″ gauge*

Above: *Victorian Railways (Australia) N Class 2–8–2 leaving Hyde Park Works en route to docks for shipment. One of 50 built in the Hyde Park Works in 1948–50, 5′ 3″ gauge. Springburn Library is on the left of the picture. The Library now shares the building with Springburn Museum*

Below: *Indian Stores Department WG Class 2–8–2 locomotive on display in George Square, Glasgow during Colonial Week, 1950. One of 100 built at the Queen's Park Works in 1948–50, 5′ 6″ gauge*

Articulated Locomotives: Fairlies

In addition to vast numbers of engine and tender and tank locomotives, NBL built batches of articulated locomotives. One of these was the double-boilered Fairlie, originally designed and patented by Robert Francis Fairlie, who was born in Scotland in March 1831 and trained as a locomotive engineer in Crewe and Swindon. In 1864 he produced a pamphlet outlining his ideas for a double boilered articulated locomotive which would overcome the shortcomings of conventional steam locomotives. The engine's two boilers would have a superior steam generating capacity, all its wheels would be capable of adhesion, it would negotiate sharp bends more easily, there would be no need for turntables and it would be able to haul heavier loads. After tests these ideas were widely praised and it was expected that there would be a big overseas demand for his engines. Fairlies did enjoy a certain amount ot success on steep railways with sharp curves. However they were found to be expensive to maintain because of the double boiler and they could carry only very limited quantities of fuel and water. One of the countries where they were successful was Mexico and NBL supplied a series of ten 0–6–6–0s under three orders in the years 1903 to 1908. Their total weight in full working order was 99 tons. Later in 1908 another pair of much greater power were supplied to the Mexican Railway. Of the same wheel arrangement as the earlier ones, they had 17″ x 25″ cylinders, driving wheels 4′ 6″ in diameter. The water capacity was 3 500 gallons, fuel capacity 315 cubic feet, weight in working order slightly over 120 tons, and tractive effort at 75% boiler pressure was 45,166 pounds. Fairlies were supplied by Sharp, Stewart to Sweden, Russia and Brazil, and the Mexican Railways ordered 15 from Neilson & Co between 1883 and 1901. By 1911, however, more powerful types of articulated locomotive had forced the Fairlie engines into obscurity.

Mallets

In terms of the number built, over 5,000, the Mallet locomotive was perhaps the most successful of all the articulated types, (although in reality it was only semi-articulated, as the rear set of driving wheels was mounted rigidly to the main part of the engine,

Above: *Mexican Railways 0–6–6–0 Fairlie. One of 2 built at Hyde Park Works in 1908. 4′ 8½″ gauge*

Below: *Articulated Locomotives built by NBL. The wheel units were able to pivot when the locomotives went around curves. This meant that the engines could be longer and more powerful, and operate on lines with sharp curves*

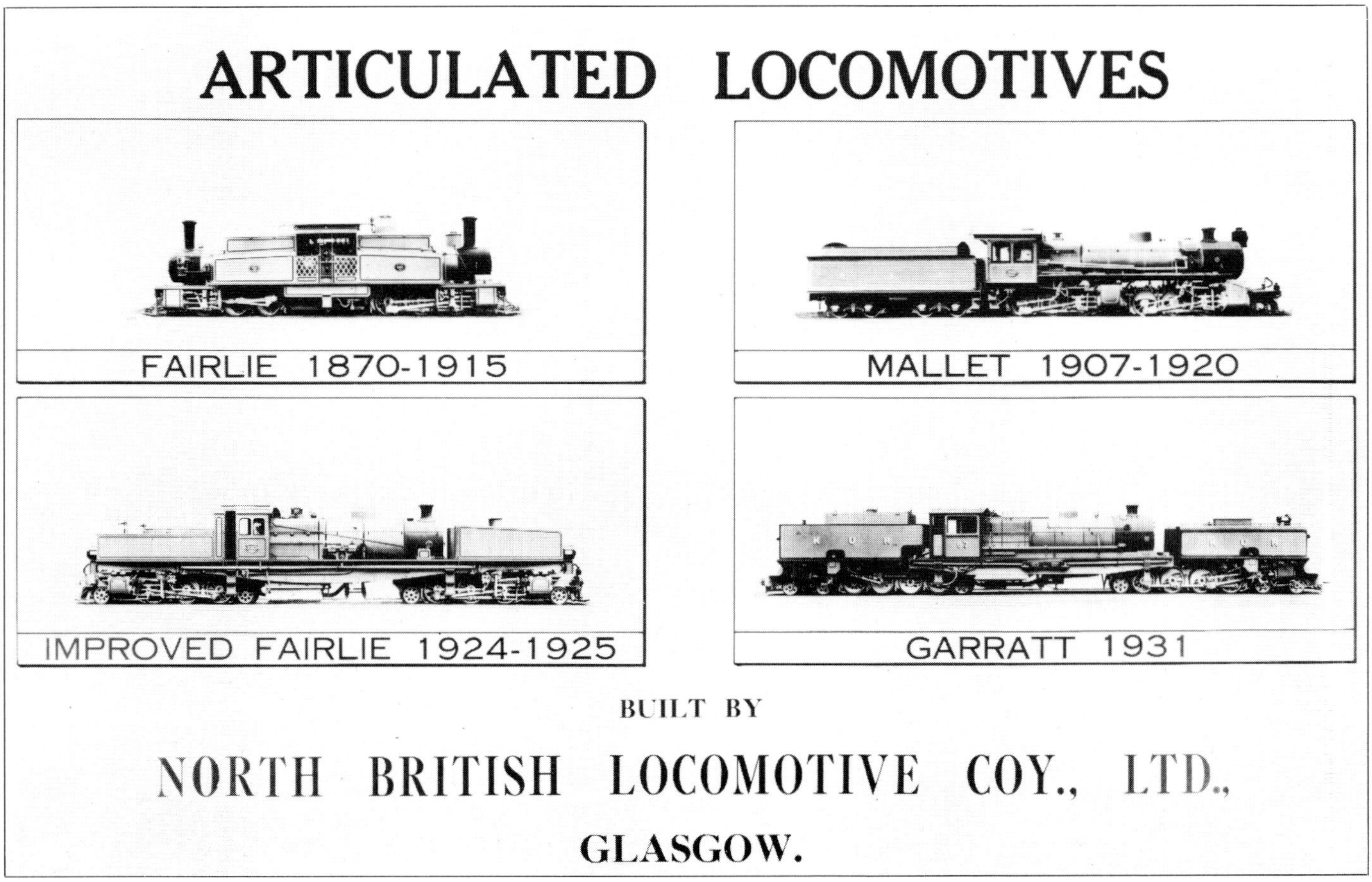

with only the front driving unit able to move in accordance with the track curves). In appearance Mallets tended to look like conventional locomotives except for the double sets of wheels and the extreme length of the boiler. At first, many Mallets were compounded, with high pressure cylinders driving the rear set of wheels and low pressure cylinders driving those at the front. In later designs both the cylinders were of the high pressure variety. To increase power the cylinders were simply enlarged, reaching 4′ 0″ in diameter in some cases. While matching the Fairlie in terms of general performance, the Mallets did not cope as well with speed, as the engines showed a dramatic tendency for rough riding at the front end. As there was no heavy weight over the large front cylinder stabilising the front end, the pistons caused excessive vibration. This resulted in wear to the track, the wheel flanges and the articulated joint necessary to allow the front unit to pivot on sharp curves. NBL built eighteen batches of Mallet locomotives, the first order being three for the Pekin Kolgan Railway of Imperial Chinese Railways in 1908, and the last another three for the West of India Portuguese Railway in 1921. Other railways which received Mallets were the Cia Minera de Sierra Menera, Spain, the Burma Railway Company, South African Railways and the Uganda Railways. Wheel arrangements varied from 0–6–6–0 to 2–6–6–2.

Garratts

The most successful articulated locomotive in terms of performance was the Beyer-Garratt, the main builders of which were the firm of Beyer, Peacock of Manchester. In Britain this company had a virtual monopoly, and other builders manufacturing this type were usually under licence or subcontraction from the Manchester firm. Basically, the Garratt comprised two engine units, of any type or wheel arrangement, the leading unit supporting the main water tank, with the rear one holding the fuel bunker and a smaller supply of water. The boiler and cab unit was attached to both units by pivots which enabled the wheels to swivel with railway curves as required. As the wheel units were therefore independent of the boiler there was no restriction as to the size of the driving wheel, and the weight of the water carried by both units solved the adhesion problems encountered with some other types of articulated engines. The design also meant that the boiler could be constructed to optimum dimensions for steaming efficiency, and the general layout of the locomotive meant that its main parts could be standardised to those of other types in use on the same railways, thus avoiding delays caused by the lack of spares. The NBL built only three batches of Garratts. How they came to build the first order, a batch of ten 4–8–2 + 2–8–4 locomotives supplied to the Kenya Uganda Railway in 1930–1, is something of a mystery. It is claimed the NBL ignored Beyer, Peacock's patent in building them. Certainly neither the order books or the Drawing Office Register make any mention of a sub-contract, although the latter states that they were built to "Beyer's Drgs. but with several modifications including Oil Fuel". In publicity material issued by NBL the engines are described as 'North British Articulated Locomotives', although they were definitely Garratts in all respects. Similarly, Beyer, Peacock ignored the class in their Garratt catalogue. There is no question of any violation of rights in the two other orders, however, as both were built by NBL as sub-contracts from Beyer, Peacock. Both orders were for South African Railways. The first was for twelve Class GMAM engines of 4–8–2 + 2–8–4 wheel arrangement. They had four 20″ x 26″ outside cylinders, 4′ 6″ driving wheels and were delivered between July and December 1956. The second was for twenty of the same type with modifications, delivered in 1958.

Modified Fairlies

In an attempt to win some of Beyer, Peacock's market in Garratts, NBL designed its own articulated locomotive. This was the so-called 'Modified Fairlie', which has been described as being basically a Kitson-Meyer articulated locomotive, yet is mentioned in one list of Garratts. It was certainly not a Fairlie, as it had only one boiler; it was not a Mallet as it had water tanks behind the cab and in front of the smokebox; and it was not a Garratt in that it had rigid frames with the wheel units attached underneath instead of being free at each end. The prototype, which had a 2–6–2 + 2–6–2 wheel arrangement with 3′ 6″ driving wheels and four 14″ x 23″ outside cylinders, was sold to South Africa in 1924, where it became the FC class. Problems developed with the wheel units which were expensive to maintain. As the tanks at both ends of the engines were cantilevered outwards, the water in them tended to move to one side as the engine went around curves, causing wear on the pivots. It was also rumoured that the rigid frames knocked lumps out of curved station platforms as the locomotives were entering them. The NBL sales staff must however have been masters in the art of persuasion for the FC was hardly in service when another order for Modified Fairlies was received in April 1925. The four engines were larger and heavier than the prototype, having 3′ 9″ driving wheels and 15″ x 24″ cylinders. They were labelled the FD class and were delivered around September 1925. The larger ones proved even less successful than the prototype. Compared with many other types of engines, both articulated and conventional, the NBL Modified Fairlies had a short life, with the FC being withdrawn in 1939, and the FDs being replaced by Garratts as soon as these could be obtained after World War II.

On 17 February 1947 an order was received for a new class of locomotives for South African Railways, designated class 24. The order was for 100 locomotives, of 2–8–4 wheel arrangement, with 4′ 3″ driving wheels and 19″ x 26″ outside cylinders. The steel frames of these engines were cast in one piece, a notable engineering achievement. The engines were delivered between December 1948 and December 1949.

Below: *Pekin-Kolgan Railway (China) 0–6–6–0 Mallet compound. One of 3 built at Queen's Park Works in 1907–8, 4′ 8½″ gauge. Tenders not built by NBL*

Above: *Kenya Uganda Railway 4–8–2 + 2–8–4. One of 10 built in the Hyde Park Works in 1930–1, metre gauge*

Below: *South African Railways F D Class 2–6–2 + 2–6–2 Modified Fairlie. One of 4 built at Hyde Park Works in 1925, 3′ 6″ gauge*

Below: *Test Bed. This South African Railways 2–6–2 + 2–6–2 Modified Fairlie locomotive is being run on the revolving wheel test bed in the Hyde Park Works in 1924, 3′ 6″ gauge*

Abcve: *The Modified Fairlie 2–6–2 + 2–6–2 in service in South Africa*

Below: *Steel frame, cast in America. Designed for the South African Railways Class 24 2–8–4, of which a hundred were built in 1948–9, 3′ 6″ gauge*

Belcw: *South African Railways 25 Class 4–8–4 condensing locomotive. One of 89 built at Hyde Park Works in 1951–4, 3′ 6″ gauge. Overall length 108 feet*

Condensing Locomotives

In 1951 South African Railways ordered eleven new class 25, later 25NC, conventional engines from NBL. Later that year the same railway ordered 89 more unusual locomotives. These were 'condensing' engines, the prototype of which had been built by Henschel of Germany. They differed from the norm in that, after the water had been made into steam and used to power the locomotive, the used steam was directed down pipes back to the tender and condensed back into water where it began the cycle again. The objective was to provide the large amount of water needed by mainline locomotives in operation in South Africa, which was not available during long droughts or in arid stretches. A fraction under 108′ long, including the tender, the condensing locomotives had a 4–8–4 wheel arrangement, 5′ 0″ driving wheels and 24″ x 28″ cylinders. The cylinders did not eject the used steam into the atmosphere but retained it. To help the used steam on its way back down the pipes to be turned back into water, a small turbine was mounted on the engine frame below the smokebox door and in front of the cylinders. The pipe for the used steam ran down the left side of the engine and connected to a similar pipe at the front of the tender below the footplate. The front part of the tender was fitted with a coal bunker with a cylindrical or Vanderbilt water tank behind. The water tank was boxed in and fitted with a series of turbine driven fans which were encased in wire mesh. These helped cool the air around the water tank and speed up the process of turning the used steam back into water. The engines were delivered between October 1953 and November 1954. They were quite successful, although some difficulties were encountered with sand blowing into the mechanical parts of the equipment driving the fans, causing excessive wear. A number later had the cooling fans and sides of the tender removed and the cylinders replaced with ones which ejected the steam into the air after it was used only once. Many were still in service in South African Railways as recently as 1980, both in rebuilt and original form.

Above: *Men at work on a South African Railways 15F Class 4–8–2, one of 60 built in Queen's Park Works in 1944, 3′ 6″ gauge*

Below: *South African Railways 4–8–4 on the test curve at Hyde Park Works, 25 of these non-condensing locomotives were built in 1951*

Diesel and Electric Locomotives

With many foreign railways building their own engines and diesel motive power making fast inroads into the market, the NBL found itself struggling to find the large number of orders for steam locomotives on which it had chiefly relied. The firm was late in entering the diesel market and consequently found that other manufacturers such as the General Electric Company and Brush had become the pacemakers in this developing field. NBL found considerable difficulties in obtaining orders for diesels, although initially they did gain some quite large orders for main-line diesel locomotives for British Railways. Export orders, however, tended to be for small numbers of engines, many for the type used for shunting duties, which were not enough to keep the large workforce employed.The company began building locomotives for stock, but orders kept falling and these engines were only sold in small numbers, sometimes in single units. NBL had also developed a small diesel engine for use underground in mines, but these too sold only in small quantities. Difficulties with sales were compounded by the problem encountered with the power units in the locomotives. These were based on a German experimental high-speed unit which was difficult to match up with the Voith transmissions to pass on the power from the engines to the wheels. Because of the speeds involved, it was necessary for the transmissions to be continuously immersed in oil. These oil baths developed serious leaks which resulted in damage to the mechanical parts, so that the locomotives were continually breaking down. Thus the NBL was never able to gain the reputation for reliable diesel locomotives that it had for steam.

The firm built only three batches of electric locomotives, the largest of which was an order for forty 3,000 volt D.C. 2–6–6–2s supplied to South African Railways for use on long distance main lines. The engines were fitted with GEC equipment.

Closure

In 1950, in an attempt to diversify from locomotives and expand into other fields, NBL took over Henry Pels & Co Ltd, which specialised in the production of shearing, cropping and punching machines for use in the production of steel components. The following year NBL acquired Carntyne Steel Castings Ltd, which continued making steel castings for the shipping and allied industries and began to manufacture locomotive castings, with NBL as its main customer. NBL itself began to manufacture the 'Lima' earth excavator, under license from the Baldwin-Lima-Hamilton Corporation of Lima, Ohio, USA, and lightweight caterpillar tractors for use in bogs and swamps unsuitable for ordinary tractors.

However, all this was not sufficient to keep it going and a state of bankruptcy was declared on 19 April 1962. No further orders for locomotives were accepted from that date, though contracts in hand were completed. The goodwill of the company passed to Andrew Barclay, Sons and Company of Kilmarnock, Ayrshire and the locomotive works finally closed down. Today all that remains in Springburn is the former Administration Building, which houses Springburn College. The Queen's Park Works is virtually unchanged in its external appearance, although some of the former locomotive shops have been demolished. It now houses one of the largest manufacturers of aluminium foil in the world. Never again will the crowds gather to watch the magnificent sight of huge steam engines emerging from the works at the beginning of their journeys to the farthest corners of the world. No more is Glasgow 'Locomotive Builder to the World'.

Murdoch Nicolson

Below: *Dominion Coal Co (Canada) 100 horse power diesel mechanical 0–4–0. One of two built with flame proof exhaust in 1948, 2' 6" gauge*

Above: *Mauritius Railways 625 horse-power 0–6–0 diesel-hydraulic locomotives undergoing tests in Glasgow Central Station, 2 built in the Hyde Park Works in 1951, 4' 8½" gauge*

Below: *SAR 4E being loaded aboard ship by the Finnieston Crane*

Transportation and Shipment

Transporting British gauge locomotives from the works to the docks, loading them aboard ship, and unloading them in foreign ports, presented great problems. In the early days manpower was relied upon, both to haul the engines through the streets and to load them aboard ship with the aid of derricks. Unloading proved equally difficult, especially where port facilities were primitive. On one occasion in the 1930s when locomotives were being delivered in China, no pier existed and rails had to be laid on the decks of barges to enable the cargo to be unloaded.

As time passed, locomotives became larger and the problems increased. With regard to the carriage to the docks, the traction engine with trailers capable of carrying heavy loads came into its own. In some cases three traction engines were necessary to move large engines, working in a push-pull combination. Two of the most common engines to haul NBL loads were both Burrells, *Lord Roberts* and *Clyde*. The former was a two-speed showman's locomotive built in 1897 and purchased second hand in 1903 by the firm of Kerr & Company of Mavisbank. The *Clyde* was the largest engine built by Burrell for use in Britain and was delivered new to William Kerr & Company in 1912. A new trailer was built by F and W McLellan of Glasgow in 1926 and lasted until 1951. Capable of carrying 150 tons, it had a 36 foot well and ran on 16 iron wheels. Shortly afterwards a second trailer with a 20 foot well was supplied and the two were bolted in tandem for carrying railway locomotives. Between 1926 and 1939 the *Loch Ness Monster*, as the huge trailer was named, was often in service night and day. Neither trailer was ever fitted with brakes, but the stopping power of the road hauling locomotives was sufficient to stop the trailers, so that there were never any incidents of loads running away. The convoys were accompanied by the fire brigade, to hose the streets at corners where the vehicles had to turn; by the police, to act as escorts and to direct traffic; by wire men from the tram depots, to lift overhead wires to enable the high loads to pass under them; and by representatives of gas, water, and electricity services, to ensure that no damage was caused to their various mains by the heavy loads, and to effect immediate repairs if it was.

The advent of diesel road haulers meant the end of steam road locomotives, although the two types complemented each other for a number of years. At first the diesels were not powerful enough and often had to be assisted by the steam road vehicles. By the late 1940s however 100 ton Scammells were in regular use for hauling NBL products to the docks.

In 1895 a 130 ton steam crane came into operation at Stobcross Quay and was used, among other things, to load locomotives onto ships. In 1932 another crane was erected near it, this one being an electric hammerhead with 175 ton lifting capacity. This crane still stands today.

Over the years locomotives were shipped abroad on a variety of vessels. Perhaps the most unusual were the 'Bel' ships which looked grossly overloaded when they had locomotives on board, as the fronts and cabs of the engines overhung the sides of the ships. The first of the line, the *Beldis*, was completed in 1924. She was a smallish ship, being 294 feet in length, 45 feet 4 inches in breadth and 19 feet in depth, with a tonnage of 3,440 dead weight and 2,406 gross. Her size enabled her to enter places where larger ships could not go, to deliver her heavy cargo. She had a 1,350 bhp engine with which she could steam at 11 knots, and used 5 tons of oil every 24 hours. She had wide accessible holds and was equipped with derricks capable of lifting 120 tons. Other ships of the fleet, some of which were larger, were the *Belray, Belpareil, Belfri* and *Belnor*.

Below: *Southern Railway of Italy 2–4–0. Partly dismantled locomotive being unloaded at Messina, Sicily. 12 built by Neilson in 1873–4, 4' 8½" gauge*

Despite the seemingly precarious way in which some earlier locomotives were shipped overseas, there are not many accounts of locomotives falling overboard or ships foundering. One notable exception is the story of the 700 ton sailing ship, the *Thomas*, which was wrecked on a reef off the island of Islay on 16 August 1857. The ship had sailed from Greenock bound for Halifax, Nova Scotia, with two Neilson 0–4–0ST locomotives. In the early 1970s a team of Royal Air Force divers was stationed on Islay and, hearing stories of a shipwreck from the locals, decided to investigate, and sure enough the *Thomas* was found where the locals said she had sunk. Being of wooden construction, little was left of the vessel, but the remains of the two locomotives were found and positively identified with the discovery of a Neilson worksplate, number 387. Because of the very strong tides on the reef where the ship foundered, it was only possible to dive on it for a limited period of about three weeks in May each year. Recovery work continues and a large number of items have now been collected, so many in fact that it is hoped that in the future an engine can be rebuilt in working order from the remains of the two.

So much for the trials of shipping locomotives overseas. All that now remains of this gigantic undertaking is the Finnieston Crane, which may one day unload a locomotive back onto Scottish soil, to be displayed as a constant reminder of the leviathans which at one time issued forth night and day from the factories of the North British Locomotive Company and its predecessors to serve the railways of the world.

Murdoch Nicolson

Above: *War Department Stainer 2–8–0 being unloaded in Syria during World War II*

Below: *Government of New Zealand Railways J class 4–8–2 locomotive being loaded aboard ship at Glasgow docks. One of 40 built at the Hyde Park Works 1938–9, 3′ 6″ gauge*

Above: *Palestine Railway 4–6–0 in Vulcan Street en route for shipment. One of 6 built at Hyde Park Works in 1935, 4′ 8½″ gauge*

Below: *Egyptian State Railways 4–6–0 leaving the Hyde Park Works. One of 32 built in 1947–8, oil burning, 4′ 8½″ gauge*

Top left: *Sudan Railways 4–8–2 leaving Vulcan Street en route to docks. One of 42 built at the Hyde Park Works in 1951–5, oil burning, 3′ 6″ gauge*

Bottom left: *Victorian Railways (Australia) R Class 4–6–4 passing Sighthill Church in Springburn Road, Glasgow en route to docks. One of 70 built at the Hyde Park Works in 1950–2, 5′ 3″ gauge*

Above: *Victorian Railways 4–6–4 passing Ministry of Labour Employment Exchange, Springburn,* The Kinema *is in the background on the right*

Below: *Spanish National Railways 2–8–2 arriving at Glasgow docks for shipment, Finnieston crane looms in the background*

Above: *Egyptian State Railways 4–4–0s on deck at Glasgow docks. 20 built at the Hyde Park Works in 1937, 4′ 8½″ gauge*

Below: *Egyptian State Railways 2–6–2T locomotive being loaded aboard ship at Glasgow docks. 20 built at the Hyde Park Works in 1926, 4′ 8½″ gauge*

Above: *Tsientsin-Pukow Railway 4–6–2 locomotives awaiting loading at Glasgow docks. 8 built at the Hyde Park Works in 1933, 4' 8½" gauge*

Below: *Tsientsin-Pukow Railway (China) 4–6–2 being loaded aboard ship by the Finnieston crane in 1933*

Above: *Egyptian State Railways 4–6–0 en route to docks*

Below: *Egyptian State Railways 4–6–0 locomotives below deck before shipment. 18 built at Hyde Park Works 1949–50, 4' 8½" gauge. Oil burning*

Above: *Egyptian State Railways 4–6–0 being loaded aboard ship at Glasgow docks*

Below: *Egyptian State Railways 4–4–2s on board SS* Belfri. *20 built in the Queen's Park Works in 1925, 4' 8½" gauge*

The Records

After the closure of NBL The Mitchell Library, Glasgow, was approached by Mr R Arbuthnott, former managing director, with a view to depositing the photographic records of the firm and its constituents. All photographic records prior to 1939 were passed to the Library in 1965, followed shortly afterwards by the donation of those from 1939 to 1962 by Andrew Barclay, Sons and Co, who had received the later records as part of the company's goodwill. The basic collection consists of about 9,000 glass negatives of various sizes and a similar number of photographs. In the early days the firm took only one photograph of most batches of engines, this being a formally posed side view with the background masked out. Later they also included diagonal views, both masked and unmasked, and views of fronts of engines, cab end views, and front and rear of tenders. All are arranged in accordance with the various company order numbers. Many of the negatives are 16" x 12". From around 1925 there is a variety of smaller negative sizes, whole plate, half plate or quarter plate, showing workshop interiors with locomotives under construction, locomotives in transit through the streets of Glasgow and being loaded at Glasgow docks, and technical detail of more significant engines. All the diesels are whole plate or smaller.
The comprehensive sets of large glass negatives of the constituent companies begin in the following years:

Neilson & Co	1864
Dubs & Co	1865
Clyde Locomotive Company	1886
Sharp, Stewart & Co	1888

Very few negatives from Sharp, Stewart & Co's Manchester period exist, but about three years ago a large collection of original company photographs, which was put up for sale on the open market, was purchased in an attempt to fill the gap in the collection, but the Sharp, Stewart records are by no means complete.

Over the years prints have been made from the negatives, for many of which there was no print in existence. There is now a virtually complete set of prints available for reference purposes. A comprehensive list of the photographs and negatives is in course of preparation but it is unlikely to be completed for some considerable time. It is proposed to list all the photographs by company order number, regardless of category. A single index, arranged by railway, will cover the locomotives of all the companies, and this will refer to the various order numbers in the main sequences.

In addition to photographs and negatives, the collection houses a number of important volumes relating to the locomotives of the various firms. There is a comprehensive collection of order books, works lists, and drawing office registers, covering the complete output of all the companies. The only major works missing are the order books covering the years 1866–1888 for Sharp, Stewart, although details of their products can be learned from other sources. A most important source of information is a set of fifteen volumes of weight diagram books covering Neilson's output from 1864 onwards and the steam locomotives built by NBL. Another inportant volume is one which gives the steaming and delivery dates of locomotives completed between 1928 and 1951. There are also two volumes of diagrams of projected Neilson locomotive designs which were never executed by the company.

At present The Mitchell Library collection is not readily available to the general public, although it can be viewed in person if prior arrangement is made. If telephoning to arrange such a visit, contact should be made with Murdoch Nicolson of the Science and Technology Department. If writing to make an appointment or with any inquiry about the records, all letters should be addressed to the Director.

The Mitchell Library holds very few general arrangement or other drawings relating to the locomotives of the various firms. All existing drawings for locomotives prior to 1903 are in the possession of the Science Museum, Exhibition Road, London SW7 2DD. All NBL drawings from 1903 onwards are held by the Archives Department, University of Glasgow, Glasgow, G12 8QQ. Enquiries should be made direct to the appropriate address.

Murdoch Nicolson

Below: *SAR 4E turning into Springburn Road from Petershill Road*

Chronology

1815 Henry Dubs born
1819 Walter Montgomerie Neilson born
1823 James Reid born
1833 Sharp, Roberts (later Sharp, Stewart) of Manchester built their first locomotive
1835 Neilson & Mitchell founded in Hyde Park Street, Finnieston
1843 Neilson & Mitchell built their first locomotive
1845 Finnieston Street foundry opened
1852 First locomotive exported from Glasgow, to Cuba
1853 Henry Dubs employed by Neilson
1862 Neilson set up Hyde Park Works, Springburn
1863 Dubs left to set up Glasgow Locomotive Works. Neilson employed James Reid in his place
1876 Reid in complete control of Neilson & Co. Dubs died.
1884 Neilson set up Clyde Locomotive Company with works in Springburn
1888 Neilson sold his company to Sharp, Stewart. Works renamed Atlas Works
1889 Neilson died
1894 Reid died
1898 Neilson & Co became Neilson, Reid & Co. Hugh Reid, senior partner
1902 Neilson Reid & Co donated land for Springburn Library
1903 North British Locomotive Company formed by amalgamation of the three firms
1909 Administration Building (now Springburn College) opened
1914 Boom caused by war
1923 Post-war slump. Atlas Works closed and men laid off
1933 Only 16 engines built
1939 Boom caused by war
1943 Atlas Works reopened
1956 NBL operating at a loss
1962 NBL went into receivership. 5,000 jobs lost
1965 NBL records donated to The Mitchell Library
1986 Springburn Museum opened
1987 Glasgow's locomotive industry commemorated by artist George Wyllie's *The Straw Locomotive,* Finnieston Crane, and exhibition in Springburn Museum.

Compiled by Murdoch Nicolson

Bibliography

The bulk of the information in this book has been obtained from sources in The Mitchell Library, Glasgow, such as the company order books, delivery books and other miscellaneous items, some of which are listed below. Other publications which have brought together data from the records, along with locomotive history from the point of view of the companies buying the locomotives, have been found to be extremely useful, and the more important ones have also been listed below.

North British Locomotive Company, *A History of the North British Locomotive Company Ltd*, North British Locomotive Company, Glasgow, 1953, ill. col. ill. Published to mark the fiftieth anniversary of the company.

North British Locomotive Company, *An account of the manufacture of locomotives and other munitions of war during the period of 1914–1919*, North British Locomotive Company, Glasgow,1920, ill.

North British Locomotive Company, *North British Locomotives; a catalogue of narrow gauge locomotives*, David & Charles, Newton Abbot, 1970, ill. Reprint of 1912 edition.

Neilson, Walter Montgomerie, *Dates & Notes of the Principal Occurrences of my Life*, unpublished manuscript, Glasgow University Archives D10 5/1.

(Nicolson, Murdoch), *The North British Locomotive Company Collection: a guide to the records of the company and its constituents held in the library with a brief history of the companies*, The Mitchell Library, Glasgow, 1974, bibl. ill.

Abbott, Rowland A S, *The Fairlie Locomotive*, David and Charles, Newton Abbot, 1970, bibl. ill.

Campbell, R H, *The North British Locomotive Company between the Wars, Business History*, 1978.

Durrant A E, *Garratt Locomotives of the World*, David and Charles, Newton Abbot, 1981, bibl ill. First published in 1969 as *The Garratt locomotive*.

Durrant, A E, *The Mallet Locomotive*, David & Charles, Newton Abbot, 1974. bibl. ill.

Hills, R L, and Patrick, D, *Beyer, Peacock: Locomotive Builders to the World*, Transport Publishing Company, Glossop, Derbyshire, 1982, bibl. ill.

Lowe, James W, *British Steam Locomotive Builders*, Goose & Son, Cambridge, 1975 bibl. ill.

McTaggart, T, *Pioneers of Heavy Haulage*, Alloway Publishing, Ayr, 1985, ill.

Thomas, John, *The Springburn Story: the History of the Scottish Railway Metropolis*, David & Charles, Newton Abbot, 1964, bibl.ill.

Compiled by Murdoch Nicolson

Left: *H M King George VI and Queen Elizabeth inspecting a model of a J Class 4–8–2 New Zealand Railways locomotive at New Zealand House*

Above: The Straw Locomotive *suspended from the Finnieston Crane, 4 May – 22 June 1987. Photograph: George Oliver*

The Straw Locomotive

On the face of it George Wyllie's conception of a fullscale railway locomotive fashioned not of solid steel but of metal wire and straw was an unlikely contender for the Glasgow, 'Finnieston Crane', end of the TWSA 3D sited artworks project. It was a fascinating idea with undoubted symbolic resonance, but was it art? To begin with some people had doubts, but by the time the astonishing arte-fact had been raised, with due ceremony, high above the Clyde at Finnieston (suspended from the very crane which had helped to send the real North British locomotives to places far and wide) all doubts were swiftly evaporating.

The structure itself, in its early stages, was like a Saul Steinberg drawing in space, sharp, resilient, and with a finesse that utterly belied its huge scale. And as the stuffing process began, as the bales of rich golden straw — tons and tons of it — began to disappear from the floor of the great container terminal at Greenock, and the skeletal structure was fleshed out to a remarkable semblance of reality, a certain ambivalence which had surely been part of the conception from early on (even if only in the nether regions of the artist's mind) was making itself felt.

A railway engine 40 ft long and made of straw, anachronistic yet strangely convincing, not least when slung from the giant hammer-head crane which is one of Glasgow's most famous landmarks on the north bank of the Clyde. The industry commemorated by *The Straw Locomotive* is now defunct but the legend remains potent, and for many in the huge crowd watching the lift-off that May morning the moment was fraught with memories and emotion. And of those who watched the locomotive on its journey from Springburn through the centre of Glasgow to Finnieston Quay on that Saturday, how many would have been able to recall similar journeys in the heyday of the industry when all was optimism and assurance that North British locomotives — the finest in the world — would be made forever at the Springburn works.

The Straw Locomotive remained in view for many weeks, with grass seeding itself and birds nesting in its fabric. Then, suddenly, it disappeared. "What has become of it?" people were heard asking; "Where has it gone?" Not a few were concerned at the fate of the winged squatters in what must have seemed like a Hilton in the sky. Not even the *Glasgow Herald* thought to print an obituary. And yet *The Straw Locomotive* had a wonderfully dramatic finale witnessed by a large, enthusiastic crowd.

The 'Vikings' of today, at the annual festival of UpHellyaa, keep up a tradition of burning the longboat; and George Wyllie conceived a like apotheosis for his *Straw Locomotive* on the waste ground at Springburn, where the North British locomotives were once built. It was a revelation: as the kilted piper piped a lament and the flames roared and crackled in the straw, sending a great plume of smoke into the western sky, we who found ourselves in the lee of the structure were able to watch in fascination as the deceptively delicate and seemingly fragile skeleton began to reveal itself in a wondrous patchwork of sooty black against orange and scarlet and crimson. It was, I suddenly thought, like watching the dissolution of the Crystal Palace — the same excitement without the attendant agony of knowing that the destruction was unintended.

Yet tragedy was at least implicit in the event, for all its pleasurable excitement. One scarcely needed the revelation of the steel question mark artfully secreted in the straw belly of the locomotive, to understand that Wyllie's artwork stood for Scottish industry as a whole in its present state of neglect and starvation. And the Crystal Palace simile became even more apt as the straw slowly subsided into heaps of lambent grey ash and the vast skeleton took on the delightfully whimsical aspect, in my mind at least, of a giant-scale Victorian jardinière of ingeniously convoluted wire. Here, surely, is the perfect piece of 'public art' for Glasgow's Garden Festival, filled with flowering creepers — and a few symbolic forget-me-nots.

Cordelia Oliver

Below: The Straw Locomotive, *in the process of construction, The Clyde Port Authority Container Terminal, April 1987. The frame was welded by the Greenock Welding Company in association with the artist. Photograph: George Oliver*

Above: The Straw Locomotive *being hoisted by the Finnieston Crane, Monday 4 May 1987. Photograph: George Oliver*

Above: *The artist, George Wyllie, Monday 4 May 1987. Photograph: Oscar Marzaroli*

Below: *The burning of* The Straw Locomotive, *outside Springburn Museum, Monday 22 June 1987. Photograph: George Oliver*